JUVENILIA

JUVENILIA

Jack Oakley

URTEXT
San Rafael

Copyright ©2015 by Jack Oakley. All rights reserved. No part of this publication may be reproduced, stored in a retrieval system or transmitted in any form or by any means, electronic, mechanical, photocopying, recording, or otherwise, without the prior written permission of the copyright holder, except brief quotations used in a review.

Book and cover design by Glenn Claycomb.

ISBN: 978-1-940121-05-5

Published by Urtext Media LLC
San Rafael, California
www.urtext.us

Printed in the United States of America

AUTHOR'S NOTE

These are poems I wrote in my youth. I tried out styles the way an art student copies paintings in a museum. Some I now find silly or simple, but I like them because they were honest attempts.

Some are good.

Some I like very much. I hope you like some of them too, and some very much.

When I considered how to arrange them for this collection, I decided to avoid the problems of taxonomical bias by simply ordering them chronologically.

Now that I've gotten them off my back, I can start writing real poety. My next collection will be called *Senilia*.

The New Electric Church (Prelude)	Spring 1967
Unfinished #25	Summer 1968
In autumn	September 1969
On Rue St Catherine	Fall 1969
I want it (he said)	Fall 1969
The Wicker Cricket's Lickety Split	Spring 1970
Force of Rabbit	Spring 1970
Epitaphs	Spring 1970
She came writhing through the door	Spring 1970
The Phoenix	Spring 1970
Paris	Spring 1970
Flamenco	Spring 1970
Darkly thinking thoughts	Spring 1970
dear Aphrodisiac	August 1970
I would I were away from here	October 1971
It is the morning of the nightwatch	1972
O my soul	1972
Ah, your soft open body extended	October 1972
Les Crépuscules de Mary	December 1972
Astral Bodies	1973
I love you r	1973
furry centipede	March 1973
Application for Entry	May 1973
Breast Poem in May	May 1973
The soprano song of your senses	May 1973
I been workin on the railroad	May 1973
Thus Spoke Marilyn	May 1973
When I felt bad	May 1973
Dirty blues	October 1973
North Yard	Fall 1974
The red skin that blew	September 1974
We walked through unpaved streets	September 1974
you came like a small bird	September 1974
on the verge	September 1974
man, you are a silly boy	October 1974
Incompatibility Blues	November 1974
on the death by attrition of Maria	December 1974
Coffee	December 1974
la tendresse	December 1974
The Christmas Song	December 1974

Olive	Spring 1990
Your eyes are like commas aslant	Spring 1990
Ave David	May 1991
Fifty Syllables for Sara Linnie	December 1995
The Whole Shebang	January 1996
Our intercourse has so broke out the bounds	May 1996
The Drunken Song	2000
Touches of grandeur	January 2000
We sit and watch the women walk	January 2000
The parking meter calmly ticks	January 2000
The coming moment	March 2001
The brisk forward flow of time	April 2001
Another sunset sings that familiar old song	April 2001
The arts that work directly on a sense	April 2001
To Gillian, Andrew and Shahin	April 2001
My taciturnity may seem	April 2001
They say it's the wheel of desire	April 2001
So many sudden forces can destroy	April 2001
Death neared not in any noisy way	May 2001
To Dorothée	August 2001
Were there a sentimental calculus	August 2001
Doggerel a Dog Wrote	October 2001
Short Waltzes	April 2002
How fine it is to cast on worldly strife	June 2002
My failings grow worse once a month	June 2002
Cupidity doth take stupidity	July 2002
The Gods are Gone with the People	September 2002
Suppose a wind blew steadily	September 2002
Beyond the Break	November 2002
Of all the things that I love best	February 2003
When we're apart	February 2003
May the pleasure of this candy	February 2003
I love the foreplay of my fingers	March 2003
Song for a Struggler	July 2003
The age does not lend itself to leisure	October 2003
Though much will come and much has gone	October 2003
On the pebbled beach of time	October 2003
The glimpse of a familiar face	October 2003
After the Wedding	November 2003
A Smile	November 2004

In the City	February 2006
In the End	March 2006
Your Mind	April 2006
Prairie Dog Boy	February 2007
Names	March 2007
I was a poet of the average	April 2008
Bees	September 2011
Supine beneath the dome	September 2011
My dad awakens	December 2012
Sing to me of something new	2013
Hearing Loss	August 2013
After the Show	August 2013
Limericks	
Fragments	

The New Electric Church (Prelude)

Walk in
Sit down
Plug in

The priest marches to the pulpit chanting
One two one two in time to eternity.
On
Off
On
Off
Onoff
Onoffonoffonoff
In the beginning God said
    LET THERE BE LIGHT
    AND THERE WAS
    light glowing golden on the everneverblack.
    Man on his dark earth applauded
    and God on his pedestal was pleased.
THUS IT CAME TO PASS
AND THUS IT IS
AND THUS IT EVER SHALL BE,
FOR PHOTONS DO NOT DIE.

If you are the last to leave, please turn out the lights.

Spring 1967

Unfinished #25

A stark scathing sun stared behind them,
Screeching sea shoals boiled below them,
And abrasive sand scraped their burned sockets.
I stood silently before them,
Screaming strange love songs
To my solitary soul.
The flesh on my forehead froze sick.

My leering face sluggishly flowed
Through my fingertips
Scratching at dead fornication.

My mind began babbling!
The bones in my mouth bit my tongue.

And the countryside moaned,
The hills writhed obscenely,
The boulders reared up to accuse me.

But all was only silence.
But the silence keened.

Summer 1968

    In autumn
When the air is dry and cold,
The sky holds distant cirrus
And the walls are jaundiced
By a pale illumination
From the brooding sun;
When rat-like paper leaves
Scurry through the streets
Beneath the feet of anxious populations,
And from domains of night's dark wells
Fear breaks to make his rounds in daylight:
I walk with fire on my head
And chant the litany
    Of destruction.

September 1969

On Rue St. Catherine I saw
A bearded young skeleton
Tap three people with his paw.
Startled, they turned;
He grinned at them:

(And no one saw but me.)

The first was rather petrified.
In fact, he died.

(And no one saw but me.)

The second saw the bone and beard;
He screamed a scream that no one heard,
And without much fuss
Jumped off the curb
Before a moving autobus.

(And no one saw but me.)

The third one caused me some alarm
Because the claw was on my arm.
And when I looked into his eyes
I received a big surprise…

(And no one saw but me.)

(And I ain't telling.)

Fall 1969

I want it (he said) one way or the other.
One way's a good lay;
The other's another.

Fall 1969

The Wicker Cricket's Lickety Split

Wicker cricket,
Pensively pondering
A lickety split
Jack Robinson ticket...

The cricket split
With a wicker kick—

Lickety splickety splack!

Force of Rabbit

Once upon a moonlight dreary
Sat ten tinkers very weary
By the shores of kitchy cootie
By the deep sea very sooty
Heard they there a hanging scary
Saw they where a very merry
Hangman on his darkened ferry
Found the whole thing very funny
Found with only a brown bunny
Dangling from his very hairy
Snootie while they wore there wary
Snooty daring very rarely
Wish a word with which to squarely
Witness all the very very
Woeful dreary midnights weary
Waking to a very scary
Very sooty kitchy cootie
Which they very rarely very
Squarely verified for funny
Airy bunny very hairy
Very merry chary fairy
Very very very wary

Spring 1970

Epitaphs

I

HERE LIES
BENEATH THESE FLIES
A MAN WHOSE EYES
TOLD LIES

II

IN OTHER DAYS
HIS CUSSED WAYS
OUTRAGED MORES
NOW HE PAYS

III

REST IN PIECES
SOLDIER DEAR
FAR FIELDPIECES
SENT YOU HERE

IV

I TRANSGRESSED
AND WAS SUPPRESSED
AT YOUR BEHEST
MAY I REST

V

YOU DID YOUR BEST
AS THOUGH A GUEST
AT SOME BAD JEST
NOW YOU MAY REST

Spring 1970

She came writhing through the door
Stomping snow on the wooden floor.
Cold seeped through the windows
On gray rays of light
And crawled among bare toes.
She sat and we looked at each other
Until I put on my boots and rolled out
Into the blizzard.

Spring 1970

The Phoenix

The phoenix crows from his nest of brands
A swan before the deluge
The clouds gather for the feast
Or do not gather
The fiery pyre which pauperizes
The wiry liar who cauterizes
Many a fool will go forward
Farting his fecund farces
In the face of the soothsayer
Before the phoenix has mounted
Many a king will assist
Their heads black with the soot
Of the previous sacrilege

Hard crickets hop sideways
Chanting the cry of him to come forth

The lord of the flies unleashes his
Cortege to sing stinking phrases and
The pig of the staff stares out greasily
Life like photography
Technical solitude
Witness the flight of a million bad dreams

The world has grown tired
Its toy is so wired
It's overbarbwired and speeding
It was simple when newly discovered
Under the tree many Decembers ago
But the green-limbed reindeer is gone now
Left the day before yesterday
Went to see if the spirits in hell
Know the whereabouts

His black head is raised high
With the crown of the martyr
He is about to die

Dies not in vain
In a boiling furnace
Under the hot sun
Dies for the unsettled dust
Dies for the seal-poisoned oceans
Dies for the deaths of the dead
Died for the living
Did die will die
In the face of two billion frog eggs
On the thirteenth day of Christmas
H_2O and very cold in the Sahara
The barometer struck one
And 45 others sprang to meet the lunge
Nine times
Nine times
Nein times
Ninety ninety nine
Yes
Times three
Times three
Times twelve
On the seashore of Essaouira
The phoenix climbs his tower
The electricity fails four
Only wristwatches guide the search
He looks
The matchless
Birds
Arizona was white lips that springtime
And trees fluttered about the virgins
One
Before this door stand all ye who regard
I wash my hands of this affair

Damned dog!

Spring 1970

Paris

I

No spitting
No smoking
Everybody smokes stacks
"Il ne faut pas se mêler dans trop de choses je crois."
Tu crois?
Il ne faut pas.
Faut pas
Faut
Faut pas pas
Maman!
"B'jour comment ça va les gosses?"
"Oh, vous savez…"
"Maman regardes-ça regardes-moi-ça maman!"
"Regardes pas!"
"Pourquoi?"
"Faut pas! Il est sale."
Faut pas être comme ça
Faut pas se coucher au trottoir dans son vomi
Et qui plus est c'est pas bon pour la santé
C'est la mode, la santé
Aujourd'hui
Hier ç'a été le manteau de fourrure

Yes and it costs you money from your pocket to piss
There's an old lady at a desk with her hand out
And there's an old lady at the movies with her hand out
And there's a cop at every corner with his hand out
Waving at the cars
   get off your
   ass! you ain't
   moving
   fast enough!
People move fast down the sidewalks
Very fast

They bump into other people
There are very many people
And they are walking on by
Very fast
To where?
My leg hurts
I can't walk fast and anyway the movie doesn't start for
    another half hour
I feel embarrassed going to a movie here
I came 500 kilometers to see it
And all I want to do is see the stinking movie
Not be seen seeing it

These Parisians are very serious.
Time is important
They often check their watches to be sure
They are when they are supposed to be
But you never see them checking little maps of the
    town, no
That is not la mode.
Tomorrow, maybe.
They are earnest
And don't want to be misunderstood
They are earnest individualists
Who tell you what they think
They say yes yes certainly
Yes isn't it though
But listening's like being a brick wall.

II

Solitude.

Spring 1970

Flamenco

A tortuous snake
Writing in my chest
Wrenching sounds from me
Which tumble and groan
To the last breath

Darkly thinking thoughts
Glaring under heavy eyebrows
Seeing no one, darting all the more
Mistrustful glances,
Accusing the walls and painted flowers
And pants draped on an unresponsive chair
Of having brought in stealth
Some foreign malice

Muttering, so as not to be overheard,
Curses against nothing in particular
And nothing in general either,
Merely casting nervous maledictions
At this sudden disquietude

Receiving no response:
Nothing but the silence of a bedroom

Spring 1970

dear ₐphrodisiac

the golden gazelle is gone; I held her too tightly
trapped for a spell and fell under hers

follow the gilded hair

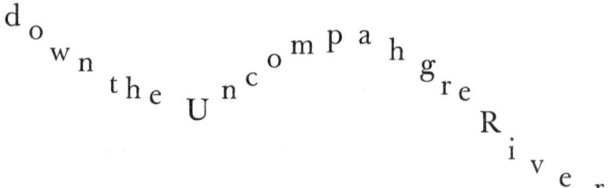

she had an ass of spun gold
she was gold, as I have been gold

but as I somewhere sank to lead
and lead no more,
I followed her where she went.

>   her smile peeked between
>   her hair

August 1970

I would I were away from here
In some place yet unfound,
And drink my friends a hearty cheer
Til dawn, and then be drowned.

I'd spend the night on Venus' mound
Til morning's eyes should blear,
Then laughing freely without sound
Jump off the solemn pier.

October 1971

It is the morning of the nightwatch.
Wolves grumble in the darkness
Beyond the starkness of the arclights
On the concrete outwall.

In the forest is no shadow
In the dark on dark—
Black emptiness there, peopled with skeletal trees
And more formless forms.

Our fathers long gone
Built a city in this wilderness—
We quail on the night walls
Peering down

Hoping to espy a reassuring rustle,
But no matter how many
We identify
There are others we don't,

Staring scared and forlorn
At the world outside,
Daring not to scurry forth
With half-held breath

To discover the paths
Our fathers blazed in their
Ignorance. We are
More cautious.

1972

O my soul, scattered this winter day
Like falling snow
Blanketing soft the countryside,
Everywhere diffusing form
And nowhere concentrating warmth—
My soul, where have you gone?
I'm sloshing wet
And cold in your flaky disintegration.

1972

Ah, your soft open body extended
ripe like a full bunch of dark grapes

You surround me and merge
like a mountain lake beneath a gushing glacial creek,
a raging sea wherein the torrent ends

You invade me like a mouthful of golden pears

Your hair floats around you like a glowing halo
which I enter

October 1972

Les Crépuscules de Mary

Ces soirs-là
Nous étions entourés
De la nuit
Qui nous envahissait
Douce et familière
Qui nous cachait le monde
Et le temps qui fuyait

Tu étais si près de moi
Tes cheveux
La douceur qui parvenait de toi
À moi heureux

Ces soirs plein de nuit
J'étais prêt à mourir
Car j'avais tout

Ce soir-ci
Tes yeux prennent l'aspect
De la nuit
Et tes pensées sont bien loin
De moi à ton coté

December 1972

Astral Bodies

Orion, the scintillating god of cruel cold, followed on his heels by Canis, the glittering hound of death by freezing. They slowly track through the icy waste of January's sky.

Scorpio, the writhing god of sensuous love in the sweat of August evenings. His tail lashes like the driven phallus.

Luna, the ever-changing emotional. Her regular phases and situational moods. Her absences and silvery plenitude.

I love you
r body

furry centipede
lightly trampling on the
hot cracks
between stone cold souls

JAZZ!
smooth and yes in this land's
end, the bay breeze, the
fuzzy fog,
      the burned out,
the bummed out and
bored,
    the shit heaped on
Job:
        :his new
life flowered like a blossom
in 5/4.

traipsing tickling on the
empty tummy of my
dusty ears

March 1973

Application for Entry

oh you D minor ninth
   sweetly augmented so sweet
  a riff right up,
      a major
  seventh who just
         don't

    s
       e
   n   n
    o
            s
  k e
 a   e
m

    oh you
  you'll never stop to let me on
 but couldn't you
       just
  break a beat
   so I can

   slip

   in

   ?

May 1973

Breast Poem in May

I

your mammiferous bouncies
(those bountiful promises)
flabba dap!

II

don't you think
those difficult little babies of yours
might enjoy that sneezing release when you reach around
your head, unfasten the clasp,
and out they leap?

III

your legs
your hair
your face, the curving line of your nose
your eyes
your breasts

IV

your rib cage, darling, is hard and protective
of the breath within you
your breasts quiver and swell when you breathe
they breathe the air already
two fleshy lives
you have built a cage around them

May 1973

The soprano song of your senses
Heard faintly in a flowered riverbed

Wind touches my skin and fills my nose with scent

Your tongue touches a boundless plain
And flavors your head with delight

You said it doesn't matter what we say
Because saying is touching

We talked long into the night
And embraced in a wave of tenderness

May 1973

I been workin on the railroad
all the live-long day
I been workin on the railroad
for forty bucks a day
can cha hear the whistle blowin
can cha hear them flatcars bangin
can cha hear them engines gruntin
can cha hear the yard clerk swearin
cause he missed a number
and gotta walk a half a mile
up the ice house track

can cha see him in the night yard
plottin two days off
can cha see him in his bug car
rollin to the Springs
just ta see the wonder woman
unveilin mysteries of night

can cha see him poundin on his keys
makin every day seem like a myth of wondrous brilliance
can cha see him scrabblin in a dust storm
spittin in the wind
can cha see them spittle castles
blockin out despair
can cha see the airy filaments
draggin through the blowin time

can cha feel the spinnin spheroids
in galactic space
can cha love eternal switchin
in this tiny place

May 1973

Thus Spoke Marilyn

Two holes in the ceiling,
                      a glancing scar on the living room wall,
    shreds of paper where they found fragments

   Blood trickled from the corner of her mouth,
                                he said,
her eyes looked beyond his

   Did she speak?
      He didn't say.
   To one of us?
            Or all of us?
   Had we been so many she never found one who understood?

She invited the bullets
Perhaps as she had invited men

   Now I envision a trickle of blood at the mouth of
equivocal women,
     Face growing yellow, then steel,
     To end in dead gray.

   This one, for example, with deep brown eyes and full lips
flirting smiles at the men in the room: Her eyes settle on mine
and blood seeps from their edges,
Brimming and spilling onto her cheeks,
Two crooked red rivulets coursing eroded gray skin

   Do not let her shoot herself twice
   In the head

May 1973

When I felt bad
I always said
I'm gonna blow my brains out
Hah hah hah

Then she did
And I thought
Hmm
Maybe it ain't so great

Oh my lordy lordy was that dirty blues, that was below the belt, lower than the gut, down in the scrotum, loose bouncing like a phallic marionette, oooh hoooney! Bass solo that had the crowd on the tables, stomping, screaming, raging, man was that boy mean! Hang groaning waiting waiting torture for the next note, the next, uuummmph, ooooooooo ooooooo, WHUMP, aaiiyyaahhoo!, mmmmmm, clap chant, the silence wasn't silent, it was strained, we were breathless, waiting tense, ooooooooooooo ah ah ah ah not yet no,
    no,

    WhaWHA WHAM WHA WHUMP WHU WHU WHU   !!!!! !
                      my god the crowd is bursting out of its chests!
waiting
    (this dude don't PLAY bass)   (he IS bass, or something)

    long long long it's too noisy to hear the pause but this is PA USE,
            this is   not   in   time
                    !
                                !
and then my friends all of a sudden he threw his guitar at the ceiling where it stuck and he was standing on his hands kicking it with his feet
                      he was crazy on his hands, kicking it with his feet   he was
                      on his feet? crazy kicking with
                      his hands and he was upside down
              on the tornado ceiling
        crazy bass, crazy dude
                      and we were crazed jumping around the room shouting and screaming hitting our hands together and throwing things, rioting in the aisles, fucking on the benches in the dense red air dense with sound solid with sound

                oh we were there!

October 1973

North Yard

POWER
balling
down the main line
Cheyenne to Denver on the UP
comes honking past North Yard
smashing the night
air gray smoke
floodlit night
of shining snake rails

POWER
throbs in the yard
under the noon sun
gritty heat
dust and soot blowing into eyes and mouths
moves up and around
into the yard and out
through the afternoon
cars pink in the sunset
dripping water in the rain
steel corners softly rounded by snow
piercing as frozen steelyards in winter nights
the blizzard drives the heat and thought from men
but POWER glides out of the fury
not noticing

in the floodlit nights there's no change
other than displacement
the yard moves all its parts but stays
trains in are outbound a few hours later
through the night the yard moves
men with flashlights and lanterns and pickups
pick up the crews from the cabooses
take them to the warm well-lit yard office
carmen check the outbounds for air
the night swivels round the yard
and the eastern sky lightens
new crews come on fresh from sleep
the day rises
and POWER throbs on in the yard
unnoticing

POWER
backs into the yard
coming up from the Q with a ninety-two car cut
two units deafen the walkie talker standing beside
his lips to the mouthpiece
deaf man mouthing the incantation
freight litany
santa fe
one twenty-four
two eighty-one
dee eff
santa fe
one twenty-three
zero forty-two
dee eff
santa fe one eighty-six
seven thirty-one
bilevel
empty
pttx
one o eight
eight o one
pig two trailers
gttx seven twenty-one
two forty-three pig
one trailer
cb an q fifty-eight
double aught one box rye o
grand twenty three
zero sixty-two bulkhead empty here's a bunch
of tankers utlx twenty-four
o thirty-one o forty-six o
forty-five o forty-four twenty-six two eighty-one two
fifty-five grand seventeen one thirty-one covered hopper
jesus christ these fuckers is movin too fast q eighty-two
seven twenty-two box seventeen o three three grand ell o
tonnage clerk

at the receiver hears numbers faster
letters and cars and numbers

massive steel click clatter
cars clashing counterpoint to voice
follows roar with pencil
moving silently
inscribes small figures on paper
puts down whole train on paper
from bottom up
reverse order
shuffles waybills
adds tonnage
tells tower to throw low car from lumber spur
and cab onto top of list
writes them down on list
wraps rubber band around bills
swivels on chair and throws paper
packet to conductor leaning in at window
says, here's sixty-seven
he's in four
your POWER's on the salt spur
have a good trip
and spits on the floor

POWER
talks to itself
in the diesel dirty night
north end checker call the tower
north end checker call the tower
quick sequence running down the line of loudspeakers
north end checker call the tower
echoes off the hoppers
over the flats
call the tower
call the tower
north end checker
hops over the couplings
quick and sure
listening for caterpillar crash coming down the track
shock jumping down the cut
springs back
the whole track gulps momentum
jerks forward
rushes forward
rolls by working it off
slows
and settles to a stop

one night
it almost got me
they ain't sposed to hump cars but they do
they did that time
humped a old DF into the Ice House track
where I was caught up to by inertial shock
one foot on the air cock
and the other just going for the coupler
heard the crash too fast to move
right foot poised
shock came twenty thousand times bigger than me
rushed down the track undiminished
from a boxcar to my uphill shoulder

no time
but the space between cars

the third law
I live to tell you
there's an empty space between jerk and rejerk
I'm telling you
I went right through it
landed in the dirt
on my ass
right foot poised
and watched that cut go by

POWER
big hefty brute
I'm telling you like a cereal box advertisement action toy
you can walk by POWER
you can stand right up next to it
and feel the earth quake
the air batter your face
you can touch POWER
from a small chair high up back of its seventy tons
lean out the window
hand on the lever
men order POWER from the ground
with wide empty arm swings
the lantern in their hands feeble
next to nothing
next to POWER
you can touch it but
you can't let it touch you

one afternoon it hiccupped down at Burnham
burped and brushed Harry Jacobsen
like he wasn't there
like he hadn't even been between those two cars
but he was
it changed the rest of his life
which lasted long enough to get a priest and his wife
to say goodbye
two cars coupled through his chest
after everybody said goodbye
they uncoupled the cars
they didn't have to clean the guts off the couplers
for the sake of POWER

Moffat Tunnel

POWER
idles thrumming on the oil spur
slow diesel throb deep in chest
chest breathes burnt oil
breathes deep throb
groin throbs deep
pre-sex vision
of boulder big
rock mountain
POWER throbbing
up
hill
steel track
dark strength
strains
up hill
sweats grease
spurts steam
hauls its load
up hard flanks
over crashing canyons
round firry mounds
helper units push
throbbing push
POWER pulls
up
and
in
to deep
tunnel
dark tunnel
pushing
pulling
sweating
in
close
dark

love
depths
in bowels
dark rock mountain
and at peak
point
coming over the hump
shudders from head to tail
stops pulling
stops pushing
slides over the hump
stops pushing
and rolls
without power down
to emerge

beside the great wheels of POWER
wheat sprouts from spilled grain
the only green in all the winter brown world

    THE RED SKIN
        THAT BLEW SO

STRONGLY
STRONGLY
    THAT NIGHT

last Saturday

    AND BLEW HARDER THE
NEXT NIGHT AND THE NEXT
BUT ONE AND THE
YELLOW DAYS

    and howled

        AIIIIIIIII

            on the
        over

    the rooftops

AND will   KEEP   ON

September 1974

We walked through unpaved streets of fog
Where larks chanted like birds of prey. "Elocution
is not becoming," I said, meaning only forty days.
"For what do you answer?" I had no impressions
    save freedom.
She replied but when and which and furthermore for free
Ah do you know have you seen and can you know why
    when our birds...
Absolute I said and only if.
I was lost in childhood
Children sang and danced on a green pasture covered
The deer were hidden in the hills
My father and I walked with heavy guns
Ah the tree stump in the burn
    Rattles of trees and green light filtered on the creekbed
Oh no wonder the crawfish ate beans

September 1974

you came
like a small bird
its wings a soft flurry in my hand

September 1974

on the verge

watch out for the parabola which
does not reach its asymptote
but meanders off into
coffee-edged late
night febrile
sleepless
ness

September 1974

man, you are a silly boy
talkin like a drunk
your social life is sunk
now everybody knows your brain is in your toes
your ass is in a can
boy, you are a silly, man!

October 1974

Incompatibility Blues

I like Chevys
You like Fords
I am shy and backward
You are very forward
You dig holes and I tall towers
And we don't make out in bed
With a life like ours we'd be better off dead

I pick my toes
You pick your nose and put your fingers in my food
Honey the taste is not so good
You spend too much time on the telephone
Why don't you go
Leave me alone

I like apples
You like peaches
Our friends all say
We're sons of bitches

I eat cabbage
You the artichoke
I drink Pepsi
You drink Coke
I like dogs
And you like cats
And I wouldn't be surprised
If you even like rats

Your eyes are so green
The world thinks you're mean
But I know the scene
They're just unclean

Oh babe and when I pointed that out
You went and socked me on the snout

November 1974

on the death by attrition of Maria

flappur and flappür
ko crawed n floated
on uprising air vent
    gnomeless
ate scents and
sniffed cunt (…)
    lapsus lazuli
in clear blinding
edge of cloud
[Rubens, you blonded
me to] shifting
panes
    hiatus
sliding planes
    hiatus
    lapsus
pain
    azul
y intermedio,
un conejo decapitado

December 1974

Coffee

the eighth cup at three AM
slid down my throat like
a parabola striving for its asymptote

***

3 o'clock morning coffee quease and the meaning of life
or the graph of $ax^2 + bx + c = 0$

***

grinding ulcerated headache fuzzy
pushing just one more step the
final crack to plaster jigger it
shut so we can all go home to bed

***

no juice
he said
and rolled over so he could
stick a finger in the socket

***

You're so cozy
That life is rosy
When you're around
But when you mosey
I am woesy
And underground

December 1974

```
                la tendresse est
                       e
                       n
        le Zaire       t      l'Asie
                       r
                       e
et les cartes ne sont pas encore faites pour cela
```

December 1974

The Christmas Song

Christmas is ycomen in,
Loude sing merye!
Maketh shrift and giveth gift,
How this doth greene the tree.
Sing merye!

Drinketh booze and smoketh pot,
And how the mind doth rot,
Tis a season without reason,
Merye sing merye!
Merye, merye,
Wel singest thou merye,
Ne swik thou never now!

December 1974

Olive

O veil. O veiled love. L'amour voilé.
 Our love lies hidden.

Olive
I love
lo I ve
O
live!

Your eyes are like commas aslant
Which give my heart pause when they punctuate mine,
Your cheeks are parentheses,
Mouth a round stop,
The point of your tongue
Is the end of the phrase
On my lips.

Ave David

Shall we annul anno L for our fine friend Brownell?
    No. Devoid of device, you've now survived fifty
Summers, uncounted falls, and still spring round about well
    Enough. For a winner in life's ineffable
Minor conundrums and quizzical moral seasons,
    You're remarkably modest. Sara Linnie laughs:
The private manikin is not the public person,
    She claims. We may concur, but don't care. We have seen
You brave hell, and our daughter, as nourishing pater
    To a cooperative circle of gadders.
We salute you, chemical brew whose avid belief
    In shipping with fellows invites us above the
Usual casual contact common to mankind.
    May every year make all your love mellower.

May 1991

Fifty Syllables for Sara Linnie

The meaning of a life is assembled as each year
Illuminates the preceding nonsense. We friends here,
Like parts of speech redeemed from insignificance,
Are grateful to shine in your incomplete sentence.

December 1995

The Whole Shebang

She bangeth not.
I don't know how I live without it
(For the kids, I do not doubt it).
My wife is very fine in realm of civic duty,
But I would fall for any floozy who would flout it and put out,
Although I may then rue the day
I left a nice four-level house
To gallivant with a cheap louse.
All that mitigates my deprivation is the ever-hopeful
    expectation
(Though no doubt anticipation without basis)
That I'll meet someone to mate with soon.
Ah, to spend a fine long afternoon in sated conjugation,
Or an evening chatting friendly or appreciating art
And then repair to bed for delectable head
And all of this until I'm dead.
From time to time I fear I'm too old and it's too late
To even hope for such a fate,
And then I chafe at my wife's views and tastes so commonplace.
But I'd waste my time and lose my mind
If I gave it too much thought
So I do not.

January 1996

Our intercourse has so broke out the bounds of common
    discourse
That I'm forced to ask if I should brake before I'm caused
    remorse.
But the unreasoning glee that elevates me drives on all
    unaware
Of chaos beyond, or doesn't care, and urges me along.
Your scintillating repartee should be received, I think,
As friendly chat with company both pleasant and quite rare—
But my guts are hollow, my head's awhirl,
I cannot deny that you're a girl and I'm a guy.
And in that pairing is something fair that knocks me off
The lofty wire I try to walk.
My fast receding reason accuses me of treason
And mumbles how damned asinine it is to find
I've lost my mind again.

The Drunken Song
(sung slowly to a tune monotonous)

We ricochet lethargically in dull
Perambulation bibulous
From numb encounter to encounter in carom
Among the mumbling shades half-manifest
Along this stumbling promenade, oh ugh,
And stop to retch between the tugs of this
Then that dumb whim which catches us.
There must be some way out of here,
Relief cannot be far, it only needs a minor
Shift in how things are arranged, we think,
To see beyond the haze. But what is sensed
Is never seen and since this maze is all
We know, although we also know it will not clear,
We have another drink.

Quotidian touches of grandeur suggest
That grander things await,
So on we go expectantly until one day
We're brought abruptly up by the sodden thought
That not much time remains,
And see that all the greatness there will be for us
Are these small touches after all;
But if we're lucky we will find there were
Enough to make the rest of it worthwhile.

January 2000

We sit and watch the women walk
Bemused by their firm haunches
Offering winks and manly talk
While pulling in our paunches

January 2000

The parking meter calmly ticks
My time runs out its final tock
A meter maid this moment picks
To ticket me and clean my clock

The coming moment fills our view—the chore
To be performed, the instant to be passed—
The present is transition and we bore
Through time like eyeless termites, gnashing fast
And blindly toward the goal we have set,
Which once achieved evaporates like rain
On the dry plain of memory, as yet
Another moment comes in view amain.

March 2001

The brisk forward flow of time may soothe the
Ache of things gone wrong or mitigate our
Failure to perceive the future through the
Strong insistence of each instant's power
As memory fades and new concerns displace
Our present cares. Even the most condign
Unhappiness may loosen its embrace
Of us somewhere along life's one-way line.
But happiness too, like children's laughter,
Changes in nature until it decays,
And yesterday's felicity after
Its demise cannot augment today's.
Thus the favored have more cause for umbrage
Than do the belabored at time's passage.

April 2001

Another sunset sings that familiar
Old song of infinity and implies
There's something more to its peculiar
Illumination than what meets the eye
(Due to the affinity of beauty
For meaning—or is it the other way
Round?) and that we're bound by solemn duty
To ponder and decipher its display.
The grandeur wanes, and the rosy vision
Of clarity fades with the failing light:
In the end, having reached no conclusion,
We turn to the narrower cares of night.
Any enlightenment that might be found
Will be gleaned in the dark here on the ground.

April 2001

The arts that act directly on a sense
Produce more readily a sense of bliss
Than poetry, whose sensate provenance
Is scanty, slight, and somewhat hit or miss.
Alliteration, assonance and rhyme
And meter, mediated by the mind
(Which renders of sensation the sublime):
These meager means fall far behind the kind
Of thoughtless overwhelming ecstasy
That music makes or dance or paint, all which
Arouse the senses to a farther pitch
Than form and image scanned in fantasy.
Remove mind's apperception from a verse—
There's little left for senses to rehearse.

To Gillian, Andrew and Shahin

If I had been more able and had had
The time to search out rhyme to label all
My sentiment and what it meant to call
You children mine and have you call me dad,
You'd have a roll of verses to unfurl
As evidence of how much joy you brought,
And gentleness, and light, and how I sought
With love to send you well into the world.
My capabilities, alas, are less
Than necessary for the task, and though
I wrote a book of odes, I could not show
A fraction of my fervid happiness.
So please, my dears, let these few lines instead
Take place of all the feelings left unsaid.

April 2001

My taciturnity may seem, alas,
To manifest some hidden wish to hold
A part of me apart from you, but that's

Misapprehension. Silence is not cold
Withdrawal on my part, although it might
Give that impression. Please don't scold

Me, dear, without a chance to set things right.
Sometimes I'm slow to know my feelings well
Enough to speak them—in that case, my sight

Is clouded by confusion til they jell.
Or an irritation I'm ashamed of
Nags me, and old bad habit makes me dwell

On it in silence and finally shove
It to the side. Or a worry grabs me,
Or injustice, and much as I would love

To moan, a better course seems quietly
To seek at first some resolution for
Display, and not spread scorn or enmity.

To my sad embarrassment, a more
Abiding and unfortunate distress
Is somnolence. I sit across from your

Outgoing smiles in torpitude, your best
Attempts engaging only lassitude.
It's feeble to plead fatigue, I confess;

What's worse is knowing that I'm being rude
By not invoking forces from within
Which would, if called, promote my fortitude.

I now ask absolution for my sin
Of inattention. I hope you find this
Small confession helpful as I begin

To try to better amplify your bliss.
If you will find it in yourself to pass
On my past failings, come give me a kiss.

April 2001

They say it's the wheel of desire
That kindles our passions to fire
Let me give credit where it's due
My emotion is because of you

Enlightment may be just fine
I'll be happy if you'll be mine

Let's not escape the wheel of life
But live instead as man and wife

April 2001

So many sudden forces can destroy
This fragile skin of life wherein we live.
It's frightening to walk the streets, or give
A child a smallish object for a toy:
The one is fraught with danger from outside—
A careless dump truck jumps the curb and pokes
A bumper through your chest; the other chokes
Esophagus and kills him from inside.
Although the mortal perils of the past—
Ancestral raptors, famine, plague and war—
Take place elsewhere or trouble us no more,
Today's mishaps dispatch us just as fast.
And yet to stay inside where safe and sound
Is foolish, for it's outside that life is found.

April 2001

Death neared not in any noisy way
But as the tired end of day
That followed day and tired day,
Until one night of lethargy
Instead of dizzy transit to another day:
A movement from the tiny point
To one last thing.

He plumb wore out
Like a tractor been over so many old mounds
It don't know up from down no more.
Joints creaked, muscles ached, temples pounded,
Busted headlights focused on a single spot,
And all the grand attended syntheses, attempted theories,
Disintegrated, dissipated,
Slipped away.

The far field was neatly planted to alfalfa,
Brow ploughed with a life of careful planning,
Back forty lain fallow these long years.
He meant to make himself a metaphor for man
But never did get round to it—
The front forty needed mowing always.

I've learned a lot of things
I'll never no more share with you my own dear fond ones:
How to start a Ford on a cold morning,
How to find a coon hound lost in the river downs,
How to put yourself forward without seeming;
And I've been beautiful places—
A valley falling easterly off buttes crowned with trees,
    highway following the near flank into town, somewhere
    in the West it was, Wyoming maybe, or Montana—
You'll never know now
Nor will I no more,
Never could have known, anyhow—
There's more I've known than I know how to remember.
It all blends together.

The tractor in back is wound together
With baling wire here and there
In places only I know where.
One frosty morning I'm no more
The wire will rust right through its core
And tractor parts will fall to dust
Ashes to ashes and rust to rust.
Before I end I think
I must

What did you do with yourself, my son?
What did you do with yourself?

The weight of the body lying down
On the fading ground
A heavy sound
Of falling down

May 2001

To Dorothée

Your stay was delightful. We liked you a bunch.
We loved how you hovered each time we made lunch
But turned up your nose at our food on the whole,
And while we weren't looking cleaned out the fruit bowl.
It was nice to take outings with someone so bored,
As it avoided the small talk we would have abhorred.
We were delighted to find that you liked our old books
As it kept us from seeing your unhappy looks.
It was fine to invite you to play with our kid,
Though better to have you decline when we did.
Although your departure has left us bereft,
The best part of your stay was the day that you left.
We're sorry you've gone, we missed you at once—
Come again soon for another two months.

August 2001

Were there a sentimental calculus
That summed the hesitations of the heart
Across its course from arbitrary start
To undefined contingent terminus,
Constrained by boundaries irrational,
Imaginary and complex, expressed
In statements of uncertain terms that best
Accounted for our interpersonal
Relations—pain received and joy supplied,
And if we knowingly or not deceived,
And what accommodations were achieved—
Could such an integration be applied,
The sum of all my variations in review
Would vanish in my constant love for you.

August 2001

Doggerel a Dog Wrote

What would it take, I beg you to reply,
For your consent to fleshly liberties
You now deny? I hesitate, am shy
To ask, and yet I have proclivities
That only you can gratify. Thus your
Forbearance shall I try by recitation
Of my wanton tastes, in hopes of more
Activities that incite excitation.

It is important you know now
The satisfaction I avow
Is not dissimulated; though
I'd be more stimulated if
Our action introduced the whiff
Of your vagina to my nose,
My face between your hips, and lips
In rutting congress with the lips
That lie concealed like fleshy rose
In close-trimmed bushy arbor. This
My hardy ardor christens bliss.

Let your pussy, like a snail, smear
Its trail across my skin in clear
Lubricious affirmation
Of desirous inclination;
Hump my leg, my arm, my face,
And glue your rump to any place
Your randy whim would fain embrace.
Employ my body like a toy;
Emphatic use I do enjoy.

And then, my carnal scheming goes,
My penis stiffened by your toes
Would travel up your calf to probe,
Like pole magnetic seeking north,
The crease between your buttocks' globe,

And from that muscled strength go forth
To rub its length along the swell
That rises from sweet velvet dell
Atop your mons, traverse the best
Of bellies to encounter breast—
Juxtaposed my trait primary
With alluring secondary—
Let us sing hooray and let it
Poke its way into snug armpit,
Continue on to highlit hair,
And then in mouth find succor rare—
Such voyages of my dumb beast
Among your parts would be fine feast.

I am a gentle man and do maintain
That dalliance must be consensual,
As all coercive elements constrain
A free arousal—there's no sensual
Carousal in mistrust. I also fear
To bore you, dear, or even cause disgust
By doing something that may interfere
And force you to lose focus on your lust,
For as it falls, so palls my urge, and worse—
I will have been rejected in the act
Of baring a most secret universe,
Exposed and nude, defenseless to attack.
My masturbations' long durations owe
Their seeming endless term to this concern,
Since near the brink I often think you grow
Exasperated. Though I don't discern
Fastidious annoyance, subsidence
Has taken place and I must recommence.

This reticence is what prevents
Me from presenting evidence
Of solitary concupiscence
Under sheets and without warning
As you slumber in the morning;
Or appear at bathroom door

When you are dabbling in the tub,
My prick erect, and while I rub,
Regard your nudity. More strong
Than fantasy, anxiety
That you might style it crudity
Dissuades me from endeavor.

Perhaps I'm wrong, you don't object,
Or even long for some attentions
That extend our stock conventions.
It's probable that I project
My inhibitions onto you,
For normally I do detect
Complaisant will to satisfy.
But if you would objectify
Denial or concurrence
And share with me the sentiments
This speech may cause occurrence,
It would teach me what I need:
Assurance that I don't exceed
The limits of your patience.

I'm not at all perverted, as you know,
And have no twisted cravings I don't show:
No exhibitionistic tendencies
Or closeted obsessed desire to use
The aid of paid for hire agencies
Or strangers in the park. I don't abuse
Small children in the dark, and have no yen
For threesomes, groups, or men, mechanical
Assistance, bondage or resistance full
Or feigned. Inflicting and receiving
Pain is not my cup of tea, deceiving
You with other wives does not appeal to me.
Anal sex and skin flicks I am willing
To forego (although I'd find it thrilling
If the fancy took you so). It may not be
Appropriate for me to point this out,
But don't you find it fortunate the worst

Itch on my mind, although the first for which
I tout, is just the lust to eat you out?

You on your hands and knees and me supine
Beneath you, cheeks between your cheeks,
My upright pecker like a woody pine
That seeks the sky beyond the trees, the creeks
In springtime flow in canyonland of thighs,
My thirsty mouth at last content in drink
At turgid rivulet as senses rise
And fluids wet the rigid and the pink.

If fellatio's out of question
May I offer the suggestion
That though acquiescent liquefaction
Leads to better satisfaction,
Artificial lubrication
In an artful application
Can provocative donation
To erotic stimulation
Make.

I do confess some envy
Of the men who once before me
Had these pleasures—it just ain't fair
That they've been where your husband and
True lover is proscribed. Their
Memories, if mine, would ever stand
Inscribed as cherished treasures:
Wouldn't you allow me equal measures?

So much for that. If you will condescend
To entertain a final wish, I'll end
My list of heart's desire (if heart's indeed
The organ that's in question in this screed).

You know that I adore the sight of you
In dishabille or clothed. My lecherous
Male nature will arise to any view

Of you undressing with a riotous
Erection; if your tits and pubic zone
Are clad in lingerie with silken legs

Up to your ass, my hardon turns to bone.
This voyeuristic inclination begs
The playful favor now and then to dress
In underwear I know is meant for me
Alone, and let me gaze, and let me guess
At what's beneath the surfaces I see—
The supple bra, the triangle inclined
Below your waist—and let my hand caress,
My cock impress the second skin outlined
In flimsy fabric...
With this address
I full confess my fetishistic soul.

If anything you want of me—
Demand, and with alacrity
I will respond. My cordial goal
Is to increase sensorial
Collaboration, and my most
Keen delectation comes when most
I goad your zest corporeal.

Just one last statement, then I'm through:
Regardless of the answer made
To this parade of lust, you must
Believe me when I say my love
And happiness with you are true.

October 2001

Short Waltzes

I

This glitter of sunlight on water
And ripple of thought in the mind
Seem to hint at a beachhead beyond
But are all, when all's done, we will find.

II

Swelling tides of confusion within
And the waning of reason without
Flood volition with doubt and suspicion
Til even velleity cannot begin
And reaction becomes our redoubt.

III

Behind us a story but half understood
Barely starts to illumine this shadowy wood
Where we find ourselves wondering whence we arrived
And whither our step should begin.

IV

The end of all things is apparent
To all, but we still have a habit
Of bringing to bear any wedge
Of small hope on the edge of despair.

April 2002

How fine it is to cast on worldly strife
A pious eye, and rise above concern
For gain, renown and influence, and spurn
All aspiration but to spirit life.
The grasping powers find it fine as well;
The plots they cultivate are best pursued
In general ignorance, when not reviewed
By any who their consequence could tell.
Both parties ply their course content—the one
In gardens of the mind, the other bent
On coarse terrestrial development;
And when the bulldozers have overrun
The backyards of the pure, they will abide
In what remains—their memories of pride.

My failings grow worse once a month
When the curse is upon my wife.
A mistress or two would transform me into
A perpetual self-serving jerk.

Cupidity doth take stupidity
In highest houses of the land
As common thug in alleyway
Doth take compliant slut to hand,
Which spawns a sniggering venality
That creeps and clambers into day,
And decent honor is defied,
And greediness extends its sway
To robbery and banal cruelty,
And propagandists publish wide
Their exhortations to belief
That all is well, and they confide
The benefits of shrill propinquity
To the most high commander thief
And all his clutch of idiots
Who treat the country as their fief
And bully with brazen impunity.
A portion of the populace
Already suffers—so will you
Unless you squawk, for timorous
Acceptance leads to multiplicity
Of loss. Speak out, speak loud and true!
When it seems that things are hid
And reasoning is out of view,
There likely is a mute complicity
Among a few who would forbid
Discussion of their secret aims.
Ask public questions, raise the lid,
Let others see! Expose duplicity
To ridicule and name the names
Of perpetrators so the sting
And burn of mocking laughter shames
The curs. Appeal to consanguinity
Of interest and suffering;
Promote and organize the force
Communal efforts always bring.
Demand an end to base iniquity!

Unite! And let our main resource
Be vigilance in firm demand
That just compassion be the source
Of civic life in our community.

The Gods are Gone with the People

The god who carried a golden club
    With a hundred knobs and blades
    That intimidated both rider and horse,
Whose long lance had the sharpest of points,
Whose arrows flew to the farthest spots.

The goddess of waters and fertility,
    Expansive as all the earth's oceans,
    Who held in her care the life-giving fluids.
She cleansed men's semen and the milk in maids' breasts
And granted an easy delivery.
With fine white arms she drove the four white horses
    That drew her chariot.

The names of these gods are remembered by scholars
And their tools are half-understood curiosities
Behind the vitrines in museums.

September 2002

Suppose a wind blew steadily from youth
To age through us, and measure made of strokes
It beat against each new event, and each
Event once registered would not
Evoke a beat again, and next suppose
This rhythm counterpointed by
Strict regularity outside:
Then when the interval between
Experiential beats
Is short by outside count—which is
The case when we are young
And all events are fresh—
We deem that time goes slow;
And as we age
And new events are few,
It seems that time
Goes rapidly.
And so it is
As if a wind blew steadily
But time's celerity
Were mutable
And free.

September 2002

Beyond the Break

The cold sea swells, rises, falls, flows landward steadily
Above the deep pelagic current's first encounter
With the continental shelf,
Lifting a flight of pelicans who glide
One wing beat above the slow oncoming surface
And fall from view in a lowering trough
And appear again on the following swell,
Too low below the vapored sky to make particular its pale
    immensity.
Toward the shore the far undifferentiated roar of breakers
Wanes and waxes with the interposing waves,
And close by, the hollow slap of fiberglass
Insinuates itself like liquid in the ear
Where the unceasing breeze pours chilled monotony.

A harbor seal inserts her head among the surfers
And her round blank eyes
Regard the mounds of thick protective neoprene
And disappear.
We are mere consciousness afloat
And have forgotten how we got here,
Why we came,
And what it was we meant to do.
The foreign sea,
The blank unknowns above, below,
Engender an animal torpor in the sun's unmediated glare.

Until a good-sized swell approaches:

With a kick the board is turned,
Arms plunge and thrust and smoothly speed increases
    down the slope,
A crouching leap upright leads balance forward,
Too far forward through a weightless, thoughtless fall
Into the base of the massive wave
Which breaks and rolls, crashes and plunges

To the bottom, smashes, tumbles and twists in grit,
And at last releases the inert body
Propelled with mumbling foam
To lie gasping prone upon the sand.

November 2002

Of all the things that I love best
None doth surpass a woman's breast,
Whose swell and bounce beneath her shirt
Exceed the charms of flouncing skirt
To drive a nail into my heart
And maketh swell a lower part.
The only thing that can compare
Is the companion in the pair.

February 2003

When we're apart what I most miss
Is conversation and a kiss:
To part your legs without compare
And kiss the part that whispers there.

February 2003

May the pleasure of this candy on your lips
Bring you the par of that brought me
By that sweet treasure hid between your hips.

February 2003

I love the foreplay of my fingers
Feeling for the lips which lie concealed
Beneath your hair, awaiting a caress
To open and express their liquid sigh.
The ardor they reveal and the thrill
Of their reply intensifies at once
The thrall you work upon my own avowal
Of desire. Fingertips with fingers merge,
A single touch conspires to urge
Both touched and toucher to the verge,
Until you surge and gasp in speechless rapture...
My penetrating statement's soon submerged
In slick communion til there's nothing left to tell.
And later, in the languor of my memory,
What lingers long is what I felt
On fingertips and what from fingers felt.

March 2003

Song for a Struggler

Your job is uncertain, your mortgage is due,
Your healthcare costs more year by year,
Your curtains are frayed and the kids need new shoes
And the news on TV makes you fear.

Down at the strip mall they put in some bollards
To cut down the chance of a terror attack
'Cause the outskirts of town may be square in the sights
Of a band in a desert that's planning a fight.
So you park in the sun and walk half a block
And show your ID to the jock at the door
'Cause only white Christians can shop at the store.

The man in the White House unclenches his teeth
To stutter out speech that you know is all lies
Though you have no idea where truth really lies.
He's spending our taxes to kill far off men
And their children and wives, and then he pretends
That it's good for the nation and family life.
He's a born-again drunk who tells us God told him
To strike at al-Qaida so he struck them
And then God instructed a strike at Saddam.
He just follows the boss and don't give a damn.
The man's insane.
Now me I'm not sure if God heeds my prayer
But I ask all the same that He act unaware
If in passing He chats with this madman again—
Keep my name to Yourself, Lord, or I got no chance.

It seems pretty clear that the men at the top
Use the rest of us suckers to work as their cop.
They promise us power and wealth and prestige
But take bit by bit whatever we've got.
The game has been rigged and the hand that you're dealt
Is a joke that is hidden by mirrors and smoke.
As soon as the cards that you hold are arranged,
You look up and find out the rules have changed.

Chorus
Your job is uncertain, your mortgage is due,
Your healthcare costs more year by year,
Your curtains are frayed and the kids need new shoes
And the news on TV makes you fear.

OR

Coda for those who like a hopeful ending
But remember, my friends: There's more of us than of them
And we are all together here.
Let us talk as a group and share our own views,
Take the cards we've been dealt and make our own rules,
Tell more of the truth and act honestly
And soon we will see the house of fakery
Fall slow to the side and be left far behind.

July 2003

The age does not lend itself to leisure.
Its commercial flicker snags the edges
Of unfocussed eyes, and rudely wedges
Stuttered lies of titillating treasure
To effect a mercenary seizure,
And it drags a person into lonely,
Ceaseless frenzy whose remains are only
Empty dregs of transitory pleasure.
The tired mind needs time to find its way
From overemphasis and false demand
To broad expanses where it may be taught
Unmeasured and immeasurable thought.
For azure silence is the meadowland
Of calm engagement with the soul's free play.

October 2003

Though much will come and much has gone,
We only know what's here;
With life so short and death so long,
Why do we hope and fear?

October 2003

On the pebbled beach of time
The waves erase the chime
Of churches' bells
And churches' hells

October 2003

What comfort in the glimpse of a familiar face!
And of all features, these my own have shone reflected all
    my life—
Distracted or contemplative, ecstatic or dejected;
In crowded windows now forgotten
Or in solitude estranged by circumstance,
Or faint upon the photos of my children on the dresser top,
Or found again truncated in the rearview mirror of a rental
    car—
They've kept me kindly company.

Often strangers seen with regularity may seem forgotten
    friends;
And one of them will now and then in double take begin
    but then
Dare not to ask if he is known to me or I to him.
And lately on occasion in a storefront strolling by
I will notice a figure, take a second glance, and recognize it
    mine.
With mild surprise I note the hair now white, the cheeks
    now lined,
The eyes now deep within a stern reserve;
And blink to see I've not kept pace with changes in my face—
It's not that I think I am what I was, or mind that I am not,
But rather that I'm not yet used to what I find I am.

Within the street's anonymity a wink of shared amusement
Passes to the glass and back at the moment's glad reflection
That I've never been and still not am alone.

October 2003

After the Wedding

For a few hours we flew through the indigo air
Like a firework's sparks that burst from Chicago,
Flying five directions above the bright country one late
    afternoon
Over the land where throughout the years and small towns
We'd been kindled by the loving care of our mother and father.

That weekend another ephemeral hearth had been formed
Of our cousins and uncles and aunts, in-laws and children,
Minister, caterers, drivers, musicians, and friends,
All of them elements forming a fellowship round the event.
I do, said our brother; I do, said his bride;
And we cried and we danced and we drank and we flirted
    and sighed
And we slept and shot off for our homes far apart once again.

And though it was sad to be flung separate ways,
There was warmth in the thought of the embers aloft at one
    time.

November 2003

A Smile

One night among the pines soon after evening's light had left the sky above the pasture at the edge of camp, we stood against a fence and munched an apple saved from lunch to call the horses massed across the field.
How utterly American, she said, the mother of the boy whose father bore him on his back from bathhouse to cabin so his dusty feet would not disturb the floor where shoes were left outside the door,
We do not do these things in India.
(Or was it Sweden—now I don't remember where it is that people do not mingle with the lower orders.)
When the herd arrived she wouldn't let her son hold out the apple to the thrusting heads,
But did however find the fortitude to consummate the offer on her own extended hand.
The boy trembled at the nickering immensity, started and almost bolted at the crunch and slobber—
Then his gleaming smile split the night.

November 2004

In the City

I sought for fullness far and wide in the city
And finally found you outside, in the city.

You complied with my self-serving plea when I asked
You for tea to drink by my side in the city.

Ah love, my heart is torn by your effort. Et tu,
Brutal friend to whom I confide in the city?

Forty-two unknown and unconsigned compassions
Are each one by one our bride in the city.

Love and defection, potency, quickness and wit,
Pity and fortitude are tried in the city.

Does it matter that forests and starlight were never
Known by children who lived and died in the city?

Girls from gated suburban comfort grow loose
As their girdled waists come untied in the city.

Cow-minded men sneer and deride; even the ones
Who forbear remain countrified in the city.

Fortunate they whom foreign attitude becomes, for
All that is thought is reified in the city.

Don't limit yourself, Jack, to this, for whatever
You say, it is all bona fide in the city.

February 2006

In the End

It seemed as if all would be found in the end,
Loose ends would be tied and diligence crowned in the end.

Unaware earth opened up and thrust ears out to hear
Where faint angelic trumpets resound in the end.

We thought that though naught can be known in full or proved,
For a boundless fruition we're bound in the end.

But (this is not news) things which are built run down;
Nature will nature confound in the end.

The profound but impossible question of thought
Asks happenstance to what it will redound in the end.

The hound of intellect contrives to conceal its conceit
So it won't be confined to the pound in the end.

From celestial music, aspiration falls to this
Small hope: at least to be on the ground in the end.

Relax and let go, Jack, release your tight gut—
You'll be fucked in and out and around in the end.

March 2006

Your Mind

Because you were in love you would bestow your mind,
And to your lover thoroughly you'd show your mind.

Your several senses led you with surprise to find
There is a world of sentiment below your mind.

But then the sudden new perceptions undermined
Routine and made you fear that this might blow your mind.

Your wife was unkind and in haste reasserted control;
Then what seemed best was to zero your mind.

What a bind. How ill-defined. What is unforgivable
Is that you acted through it all as though your mind

Were some fine instrument that justifies conceit.
But O, my clueless friend, you do not know your mind.

April 2006

Prairie Dog Boy ran from place to place
In search of mother and father
Under the wide blue sky,
The wide blank sky.

Mother moon and father sun together shone,
But the sky was wide,
The sky was blank.

Prairie Dog Boy searched for earth mother and earth
    father,
The two who made his nest,
The two warm ones,
The ones like him, his chest, his head.

Sun father and moon mother were big and strong,
All-mother and all-father,
But the deep black sky and bland blue sky were not like
    him.

Prairie Dog Boy ran from place to place
Sniffing for warmth.

February 2007

Names

I have two sons I call by each other's name now and then,
Especially when we are all together. Puzzled, they
Glance up at me, and my wife silently wonders again how
My memory can be so bad. Many times I haven't
Even noticed the mistake. It's worse when my brothers are there,
Worse still if my nephews—their sons and my sisters'—are in
The mix, too. I'll pile name upon name in a tongue-twisted
Attempt to light upon the right one. They ask me chaffing
If I'm aging, if my memory's gone, whether the slip
Is a sign of secret preference, or a lack
Of attention, or am I so self-engrossed that I don't
Notice the people around me? Still worse is that my sons
Have different mothers who share half a name. You may well
Imagine that from time to time I pause before I speak,
And often address my wife with commonplace endearments.

I reply by way of acquittal that I'm just like my
Mother, who runs through a few names before finding the one
That fits the kid in question. Don't forget, they say, we always
Laugh at her, and anyway the likeness does not excuse you.

I can not admit in company what is at the root:
You mingle in my mind, my heart, my soul: You seem to be
All parts of me: The one, the other, both and all: Though each
Unique and irreplaceable, each appreciated
For your particularity, each known to me indeed
As you alone: In my inmost apprehension you are
Facets of the love that emanates around me, a love
Which overwhelms my faculty of discrimination.
I know very well who is who but often a surfeit
Of happiness addles me.
Loving and beloved ones, dear family,
Forgive me for calling you by the wrong name.

March 2007

I was a poet of the average, the goddamned average, an
    average goddamned poet,
If a poet at all,
And not simply one of the ones who wouldn't shut his yap
—As if that made some claim upon the world to listen
Or some long-suffering companion to console.

April 2008

The bees that dart among the clover
May not know they hover over it,
But have at least a purpose I do not,
Unless it be observing them.

Supine beneath the dome wherein the planets wheel,
I feel unceasing motion both within myself
And far beyond the ever-growing bubble of the light—
Collision, expectation and desire—
If only I could say one day:
Enough, I will repose a while
Outside this endless whirlpool;
And slip with ease between the froth of life
And calm, unmoving state of death
To rest in stillness,
And when refreshed rejoin the swirling gyre.

September 2011

My dad awakens on arriving home
and hobbles to the bedroom where he puts
away his things, pulls on pajamas, asks
my sister for the time. Two-thirty. I'll
go to bed, he says. But Dad, it's afternoon,
look, it's light outside. Oh no, he says,
with a note of disappointment.
November's lowering sun confuses him.
Afternoon becomes slow night. Actions once
engrossing, even simple acts performed
without thought are forgotten, although he
always remembers to say: I love you.

December 2012

Sing to me of something new,
My heart spoke to my soul,
These fables that you bring to me
Are often told and known to all—
    War's horrors are well documented,
    Brevity of life lamented,
    Melancholy testamented,
    Young man crossing cataract or fire
    To reach his object of desire,
    Maiden sighing yearningly
    Awaiting one to set her free,
    Bittersweet parental pride
    In children's growth from infancy—
To hear again these commonplaces,
Though deeply felt and never better worded,
Is wearisome and languorous.
Speak to me of something yet unheard.

Then feel for me a thing not felt before,
My soul responded,
For I am bound by what I find
And that arrives through you.

2013

Hearing Loss

    I lost my hearing for two days when swimming five feet deep forced a buildup of wax forced into my ears. I couldn't hear what was said, I could barely hear the piano I played, and my skull vibrated when I brushed my teeth.
    Luckily my doctor could see me the second day after. As I drove to the appointment I couldn't hear the usual sounds so I drove by instrument. He flushed my ear three times with a shiny metal syringe the size of my forearm. Brown effluent four times, and the fifth time he said Aha! And in that instant I heard the air grille overhead clatter and the syringe clank and the water drip onto the floor, the click of his door behind me, my key in the lock of my car, the window winder ticking down, and since then I've been hoping to hear birds chirp, leaves rustle and lizards scrabble through the grass, but I hear what there is to hear—whoosh of wheels on pavement, rattle of a zipper on my briefcase, a bike chain squeak, truck brakes squeal—machinery everywhere.

After the Show

When we die we'll take off the costumes and makeup
And join the cast already behind the curtain
(Fathers, mothers, husbands, wives, friends dear and distant)
Out of the glaring light that kept us ever
At the center of attention as we carefully
Constructed characters to play; relaxed now,
Strolling two by three or laughing in small groups
About the silliness we saw and how we felt
Beneath the pose and what we really meant but were afraid
Or had no time or could not find the words to say,
Welcoming with joy the new arrivals from on stage.

August 2013

It seems that a bishop of Limerick composed church music during the period of Tartar invasions. Anxiety that his congregation might be assaulted during mass by a horde bent on mayhem, murder, and rape was compounded by fear of the blasphemy committed if a hymn once begun was not completed, even to take up arms for defense. The bishop contrived to spare himself and his flock from martyrdom on the one hand and damnation on the other by writing short stanzas which could if necessary be chanted in double time. His versification was widely imitated and he himself was commemorated:

There once was a sinner from Sodom
Who hymned to the Lord songs to laud him.
Faced with invasion
From sources Eurasian
He sang fast to safeguard his bottom.

***

There once was a young man from France
Who thought he had ants in his pants.
Though indeed attacked,
Twas incest in fact–
The hands in his pants were his aunt's.

There once was a gay from Nebraska
Who traveled to play in Alaska.
The Eskimos there
Laid nothing but bear,
So he came back by way of the Castro.

There was a young lady from Frisco
Who took life for a bottle of Crisco.
When she found it was hard,
Less like oil than like lard,
She recoiled and forsook it quite brisko.

Fragments

    through land desolate
and ages barren to the mind of men

1972

Grass is green
Roses are red
If you get pregnant
You're better off dead

February 1973

I'm addicted and afflicted with a sense of malproportion,
For the woman that I love is filing for abortion.

August 1974

You sit there and sulk
Head under your skull cap

Fall 1974

My rough avowals are not good enough

April 2001

Behind us a story but half understood
To the sides a perspective of mist
Ahead the unknown and no heaven to help

October 2002

www.ingramcontent.com/pod-product-compliance
Lightning Source LLC
Chambersburg PA
CBHW031402040426
42444CB00005B/394